Stre

Riley

Street Dogs

Drawings and notes from the street books of artist Harold Riley

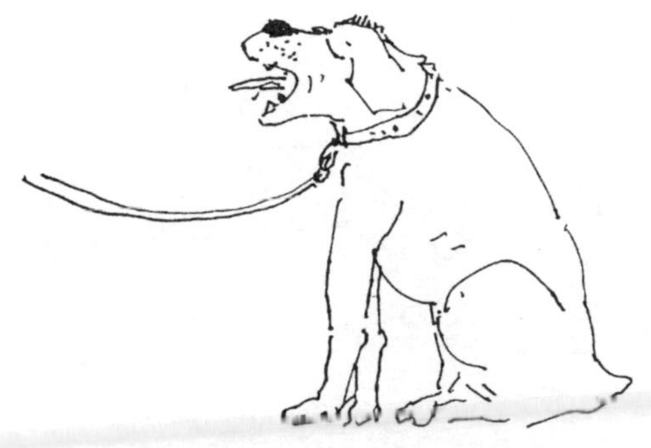

Millrace for The Riley Archive

First published in Great Britain in the year 2000 by
Millrace, 2a Leafield Road, Disley, Cheshire SK12 2JF
for The Riley Archive.

ISBN: 1 902173 090

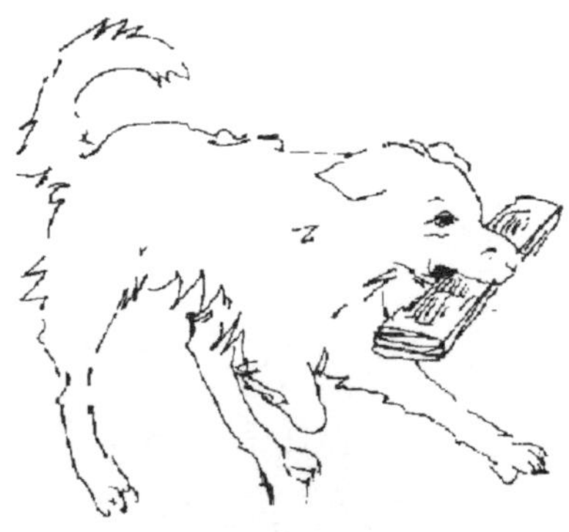

Typeset in Baskerville BE Regular.
Printed and bound in Great Britain by
The Peak Press Company, Chapel-en-le-Frith, Derbyshire.

For dog lovers everywhere

Contents

Introduction 1

Jack the Happy Dog 4
Ellor Street, Salford, 1969
Jack the Ripper 6
off Regent Road, Salford, 1967
Freewheel the Corgi 8
Brindle Heath, circa 1955
The Cross-Eyed Dancing Dog 10
Outside 'The Fox', Regent Road, 1961
The Three-Legged Dog 12
Norway Street, Seedley, 1980
Ben the Bin Dog 14
Frederick Road, Salford, 1987
Dicky the Somersaulter 16
Brindley Street, 1965
Clark the Bulldog 18
Nan Nook Road, Manchester, 1963
Nat the Panter 20
Scroggins Lane, Urmston, 1954
Sissy, a Dancing Dog 22
Southern Street, Seedley, 1971
Billy the Builder's Dog 24
Kara Street, Salford, 1963

The Roof Dog 26
Liverpool Street, 1955
Doo-Lali 28
Boardman Street, Eccles, 1978
The Chair Dog 30
Ellor Street, 1949
Bella the Icecream Snatcher 32
Radford Street, Kersal, 1961
Norris, a Sad Dog 34
Eavesford Walk, Salford, 1962
Noddy 36
Colyhurst, Manchester, 1972
Pirate 38
'Waggon & Horses', Eccles, circa 1950
Barlow the Policeman's Dog 40
Bazaar Street, Salford, 1961
Dog with his Head in a Hole 42
Stott Lane, Salford, 1962
Jago the Sniffer 44
Eccles Pet Shop, 1961
Gilbert the Newsagent's Dog 46
Heap Street, 1962
Jip the Jumping Dog 48
Derby Road, Seedley, 1959
A Thin Dog 50
Irlams o' th' Height, 1969
The Chimney Sweep's Dog 52
Tootal Drive, Weaste, 1971
About the Artist 55

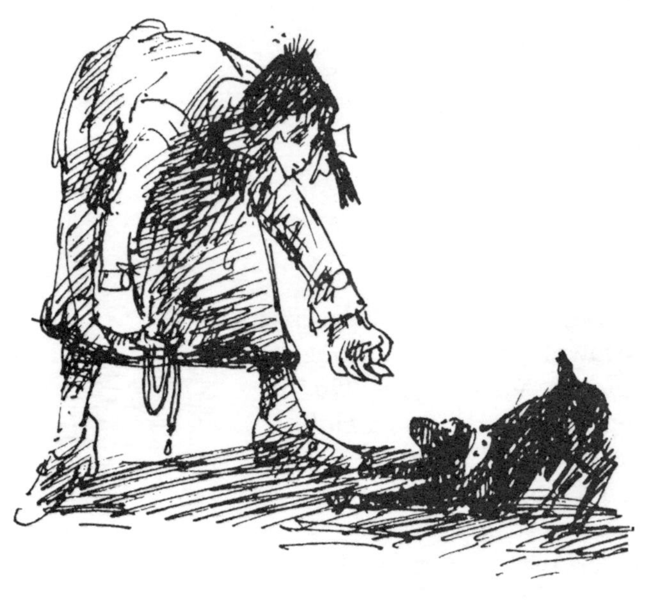

'Cum ere' ya little sod!'

Introduction

This book is a collection of twenty-five dogs from the hundreds in my sketchbooks. The dogs come from the streets of the town where I have lived all my life. They cover pages or margins of the many work-books I have made in the city. Brief notes sometimes accompanied the dogs and, although they will probably mean little to those who live outside Lancashire in England, I recorded the place and date for my own interest.

July 2000

The Dogs

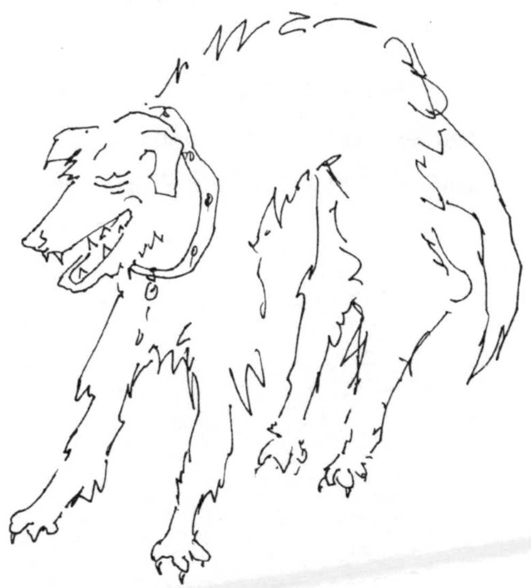

Jack the Happy Dog. Didn't do much except sit on the corner of Ellor Street by the lamp-post and smile. Didn't seem to need anybody. Well known in Hankey Park – Walter Greenwood said he must be very old because he remembered him. Don't know that he could have – his master said he was only five years old.

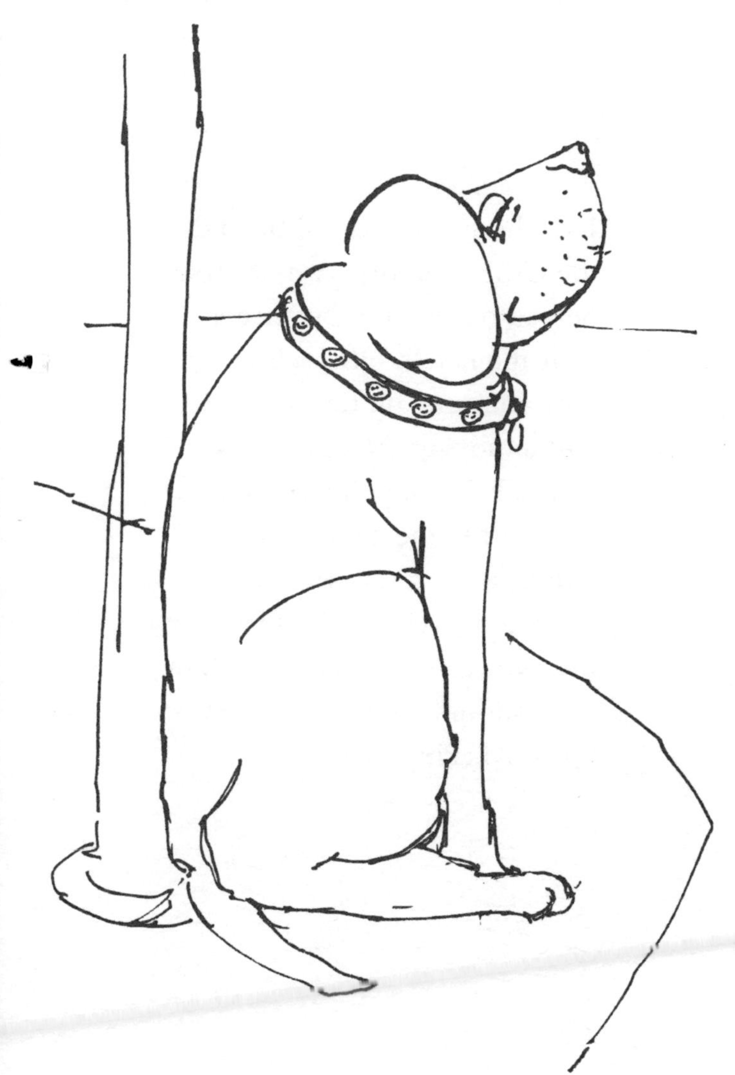

Jack the Ripper. Lived behind the Croft Laundry. A nasty sod. Stayed outside the butcher's, near the health offices. Spent his time squirting on the shop front and annoying the customers. Had a habit of grabbing rain-coats. At home he attacked almost everybody who passed their house. He was watched by the two cats who lived with him – he adored the cats and was forever licking them!

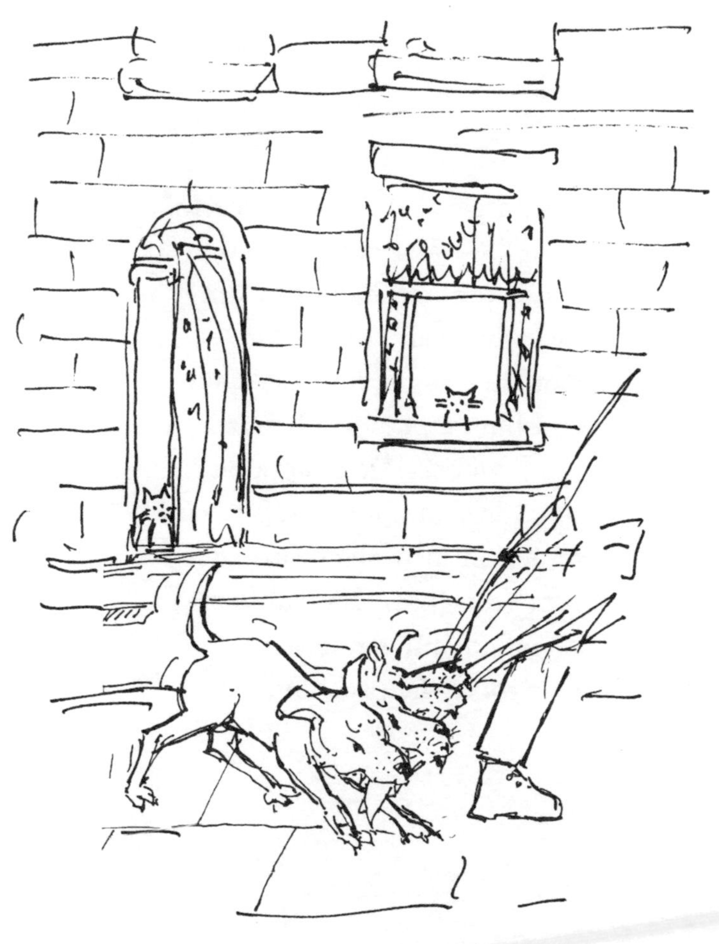

Freewheel the Corgi. At least, I think he was a corgi. Lived in Pendleton and had been run over by a car. His master wouldn't have him destroyed and built a platform between two pram wheels. He strapped the dog's legs to the contraption and took him for walks. Kids called him Freewheel. He was very dignified and gentle – so everybody helped him.

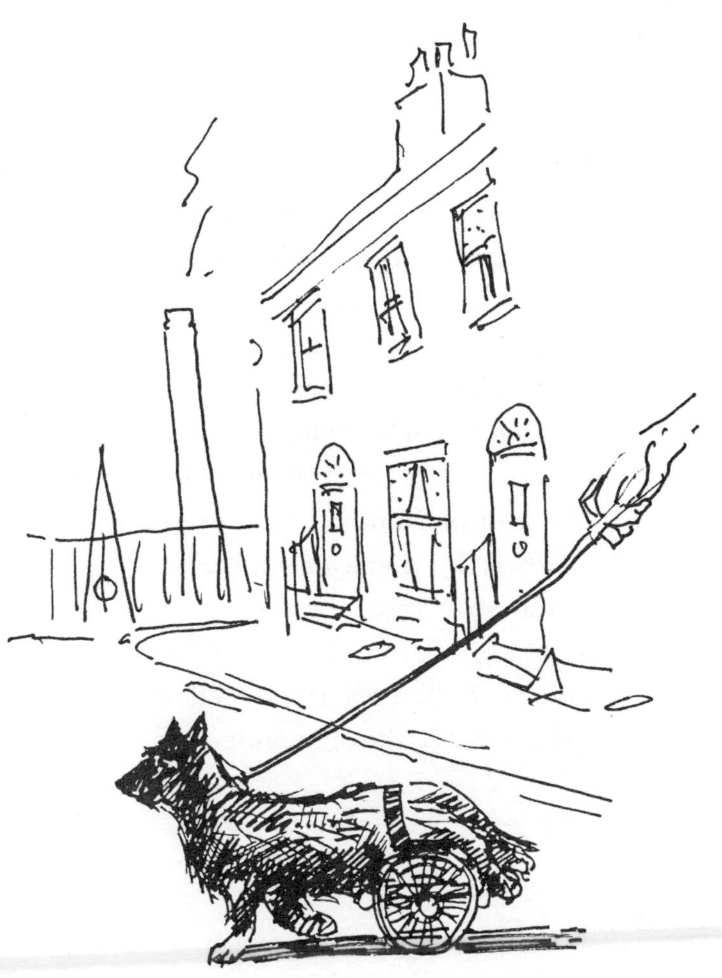

The Cross-Eyed Dancing Dog. Belonged to Jack Hall's Dancing Dog Band. Jack Hall was a one-man band. He had a group of dogs who started jumping around when he banged his drum. This cross-eyed one was the best performer. I took Martin Milner, the leader of the Hallé Orchestra, to see the dogs dancing. He said they could 'do a turn' at the Free Trade Hall with John Barbirolli conducting.

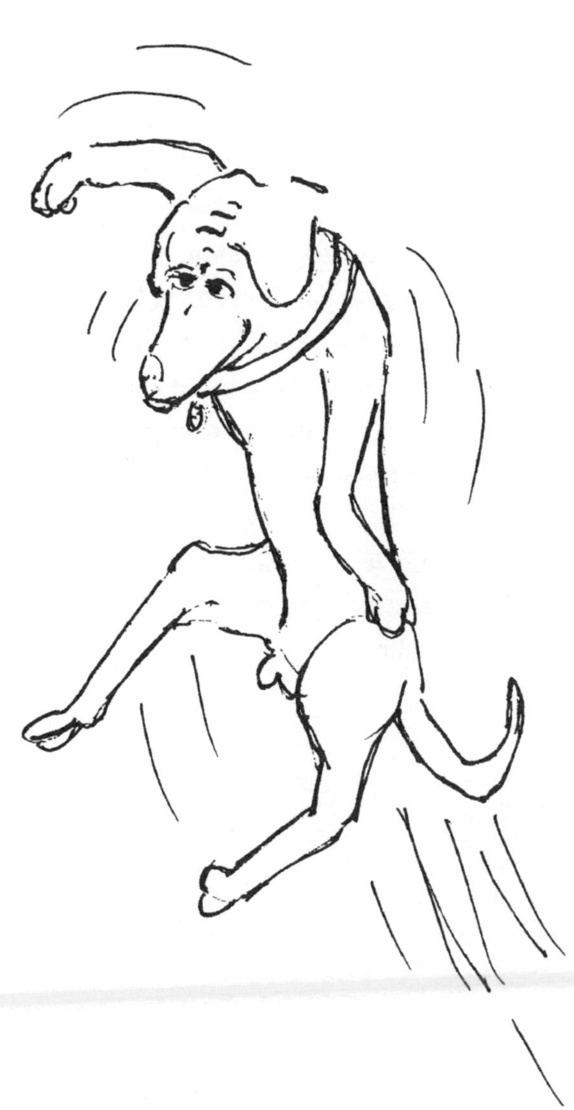

The Three-Legged Dog. Went to a newsagent on Liverpool Street for the *Manchester Evening News.* Rain or shine. You could tell the time by the time the dog passed. His owner was a bus driver who lived alone with the dog. He was a reclusive man but loved the dog greatly. Never knew the dog's name.

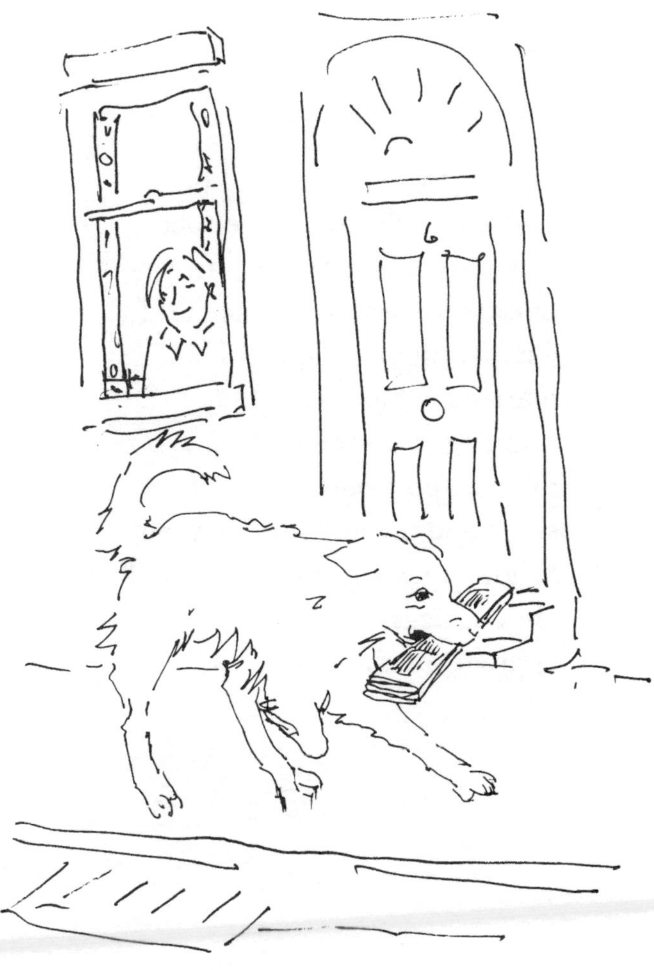

Ben. A dog who guarded the dustbins at the top of the road near Broad Street. The bins were outside the transport café and he guarded them jealously. His place gave him the right to rummage for scraps. We used the transport café as a 'tuck shop' and the Salford Grammar School boys knew Ben very well. He was aggressive if you approached the bins.

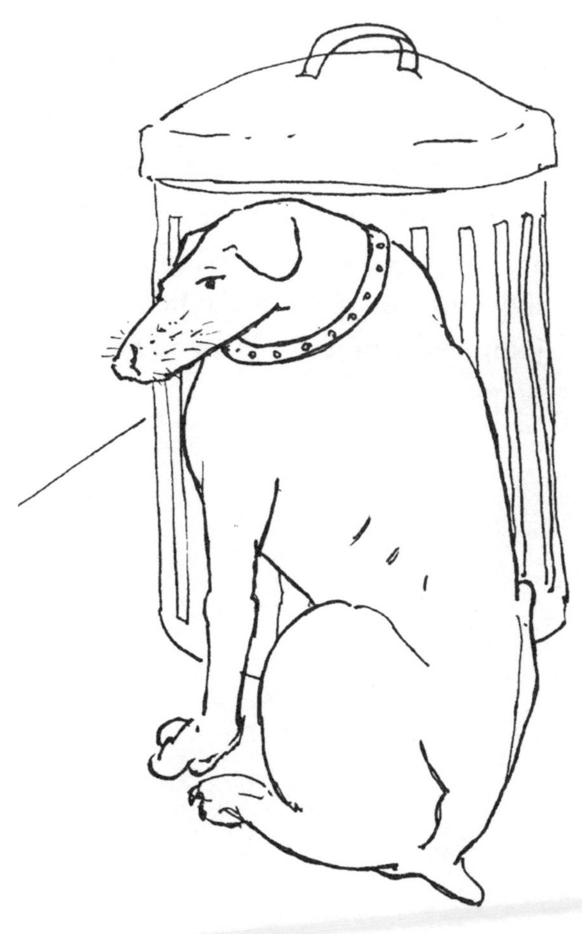

Dicky. A dachshund who lived in Brindley Street and turned somersaults. He belonged to a little girl who could make him jump every time she clapped her hands.

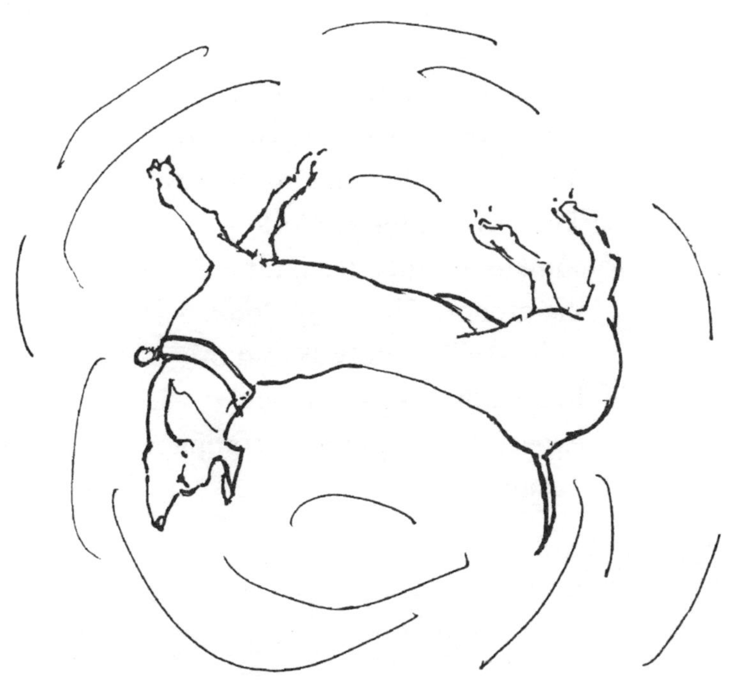

Clark the Bulldog. Well known for making smells. He could be heard doing it a long way away. The force of the explosion sometimes lifted his hind legs off the ground. He always looked rather sullen and was told off frequently – as you might expect. He got rather a complex, I think.

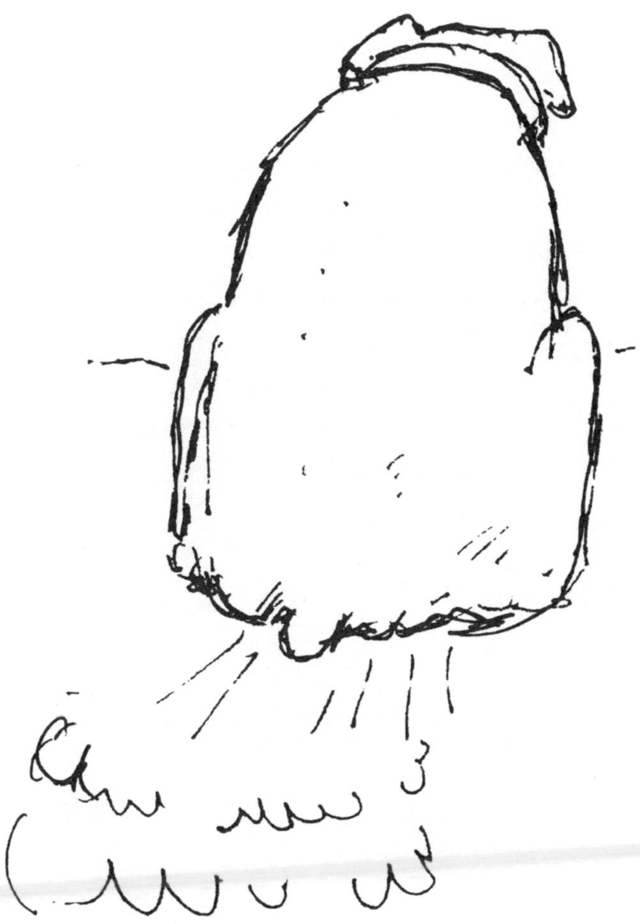

Nat the Panter. Was always panting. Panted to the front, sideways and even tried to pant over his shoulder, backwards. Looked as if he was laughing all the time. Lived not far from Barton Aerodrome and the owner said Nat was affected by the noise of the planes flying over the house.

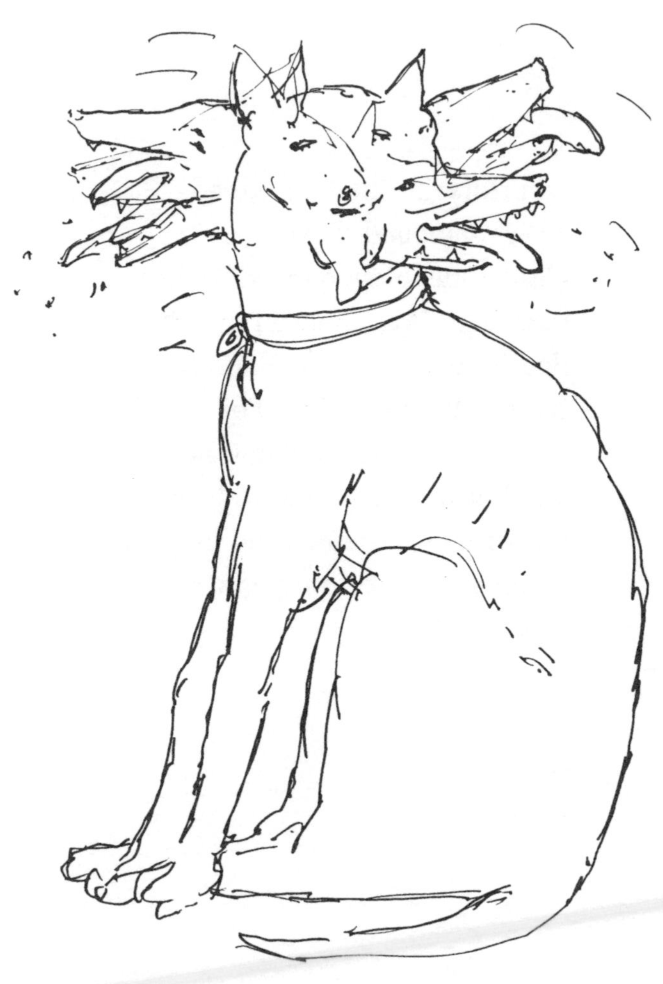

Sad story. A little dog called Sissy. Belonged to Mrs Castledine. Sissy danced on her back legs. Was attacked by a big dog from White Street and badly bitten. Was put down. Polly Castledine never had another dog but was very kind to Jimmy the window-cleaner, who lived at Number 2, next to my grand-mother's house.

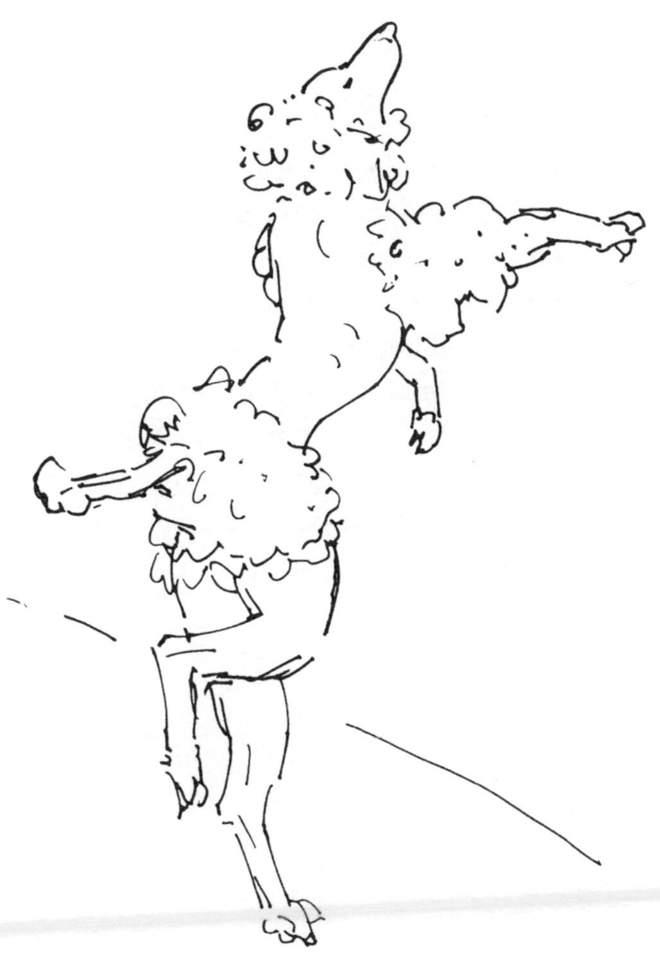

Billy the Builder's Dog. Was supposed to look after the builder's yard in Kara Street. He squeezed through a hole in the fence and peeped round the corner until he saw Bill Corrie, the builder, coming back. Then he ran back into the yard and started barking as if he'd been on guard all the time.

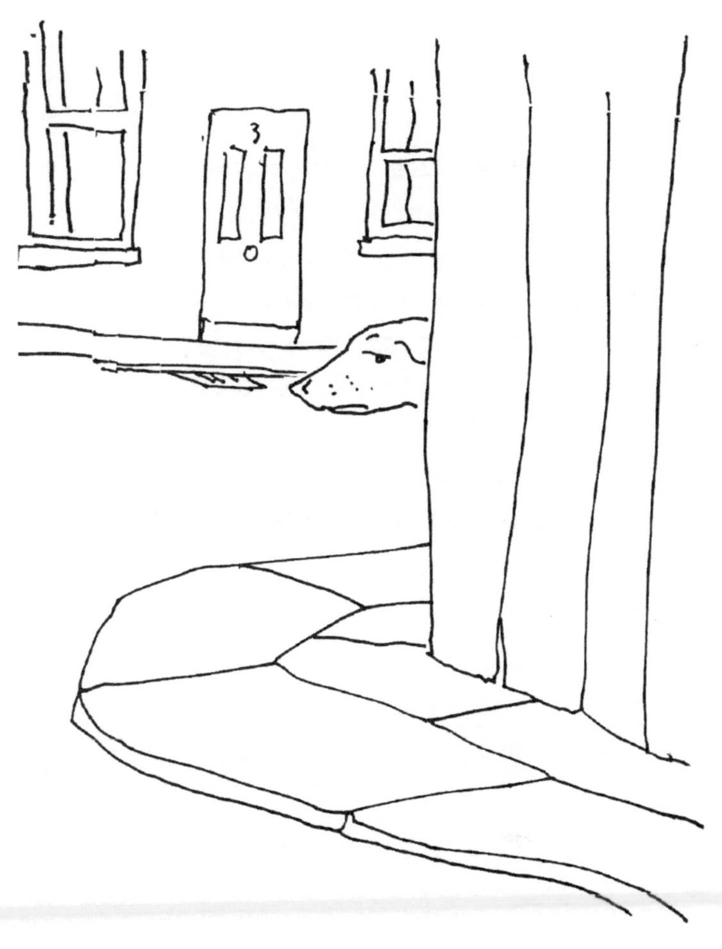
3

The Roof Dog. A tiny mongrel who lived on the roof of a raincoat factory in Liverpool Street. The owner, Mr Hyman, said the dog only answered to Yiddish. He fell off the roof when Mr Hyman was in Israel, getting married. I took the dog to the vet and he got better.

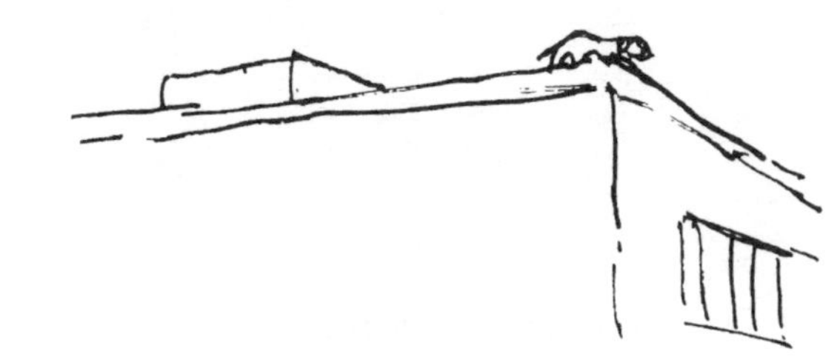

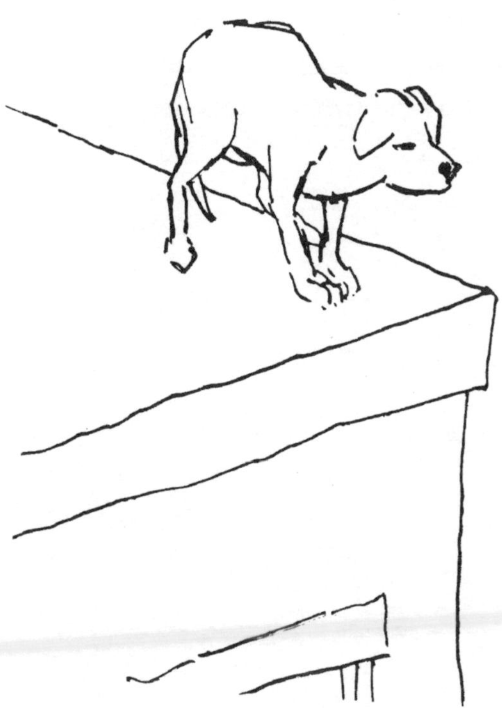

Dog called Doo-Lali. Delightful little sausage dog. Lived in Boardman Street. Always jumping up on its hind legs and licking your hands. Was badly abused by its owner, a bus driver from Eccles.

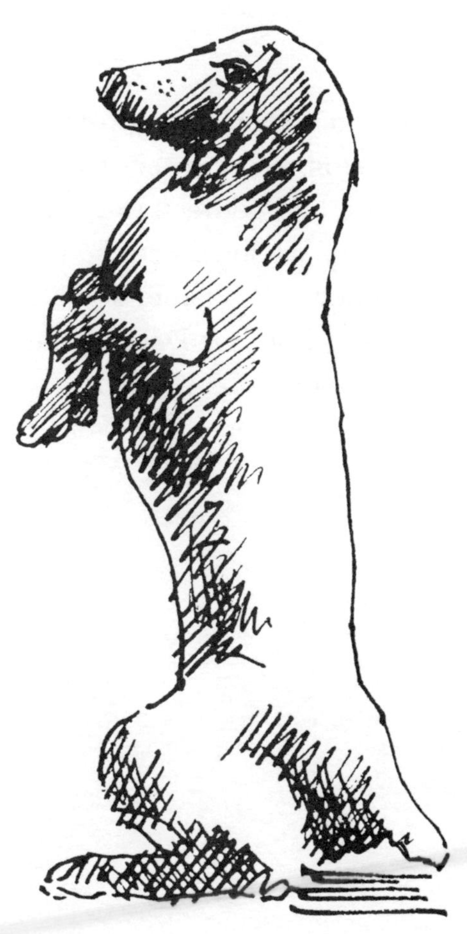

The Chair Dog. A dog from Pendleton whose owner would balance him between two chairs, where he wobbled until he was lifted down. 'A shame,' said Mrs Appleby from the Dogs Home. 'His owner's a barmy sod!'

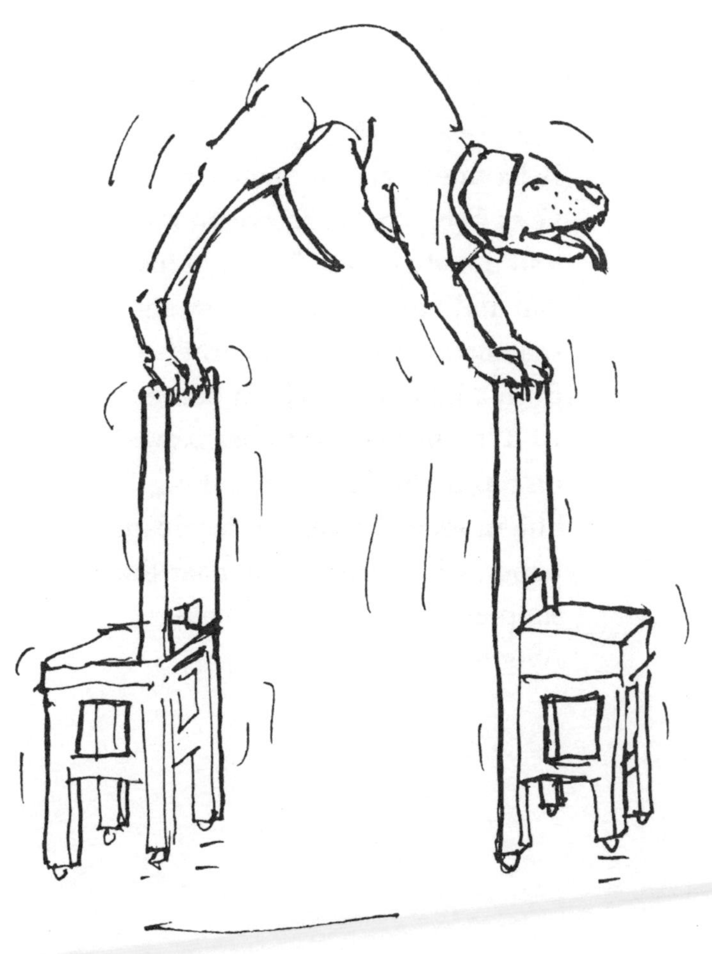

Bella the Icecream Snatcher. Peter Schiavo, the icecream man, told me about her. I went in his van and he showed me how she snatched the icecream cornet from a little boy and ran home with it. She ate it with her paws on top of the fence – watching. She mooched about for icecream paper, which she licked, near the shop at the top of Brookfield Avenue.

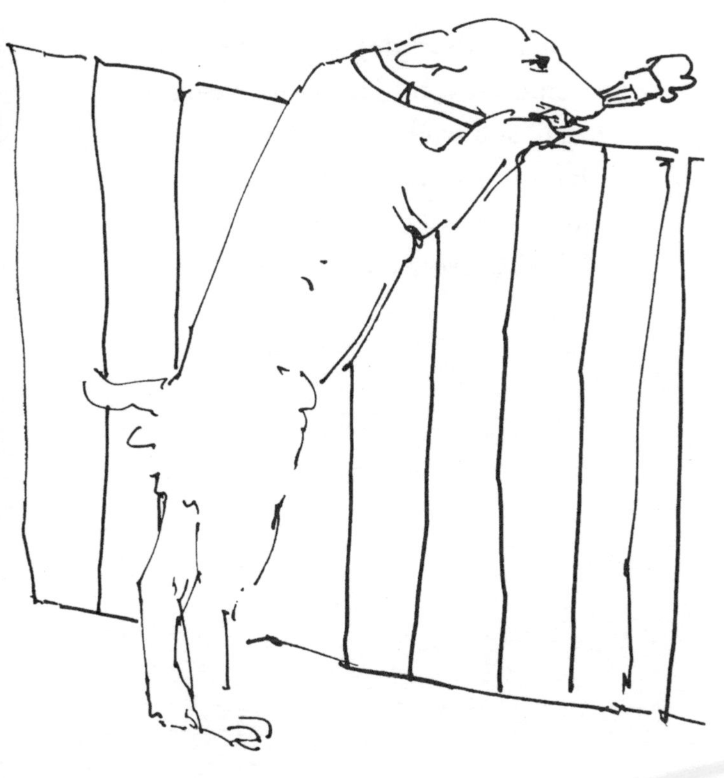

Norris. A sad dog that nobody bothered with. He sat for years against a wall at the end of Eavesford Walk. I was told a lorry ran over him. He was killed chasing a cat across the street.

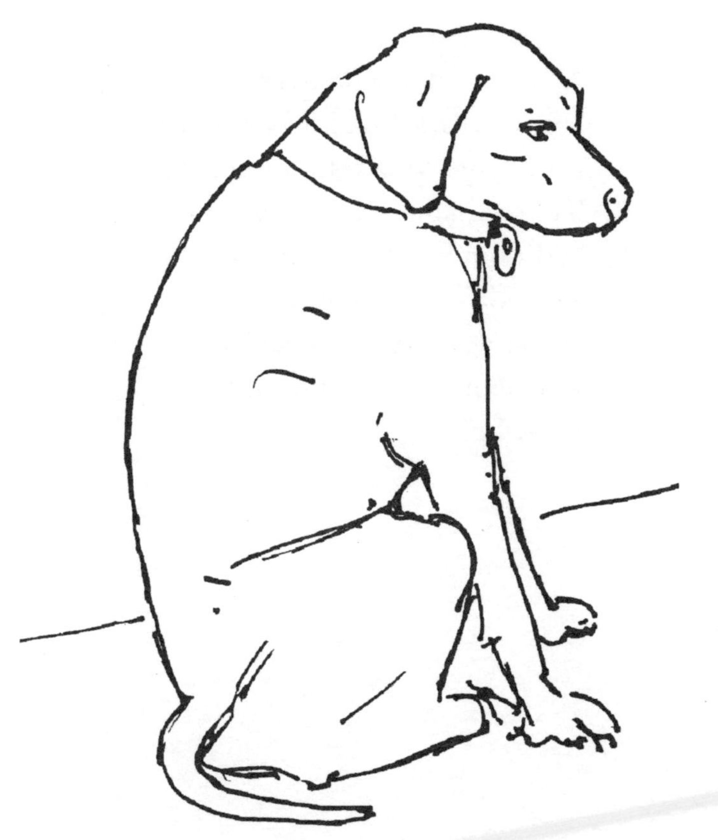

Noddy. A dog who lived in Seedley Park Road, where there were large Victorian houses. He had the habit of jumping from a bedroom window – usually after a cat, or when he was encouraged by the local lads, who shouted at him from the street below.

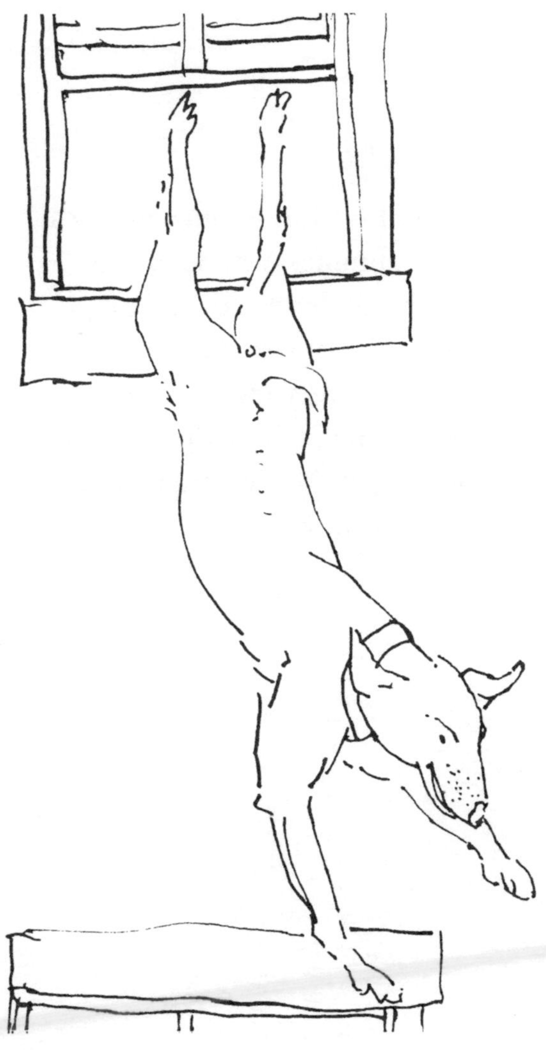

Pirate. Lived in Boothstown near the coal mine. A miner's dog who reminded his owner of Long John Silver. Waited patiently every night except Sunday, tied to a railing outside the Waggon & Horses, a pub in Peel Green, Eccles.

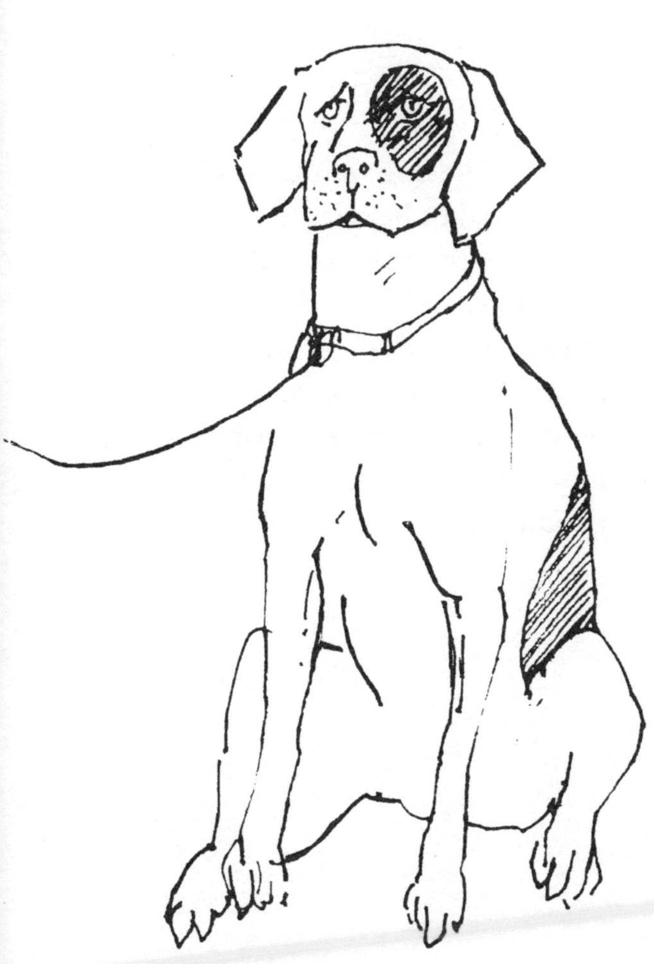

Barlow. The dog who sat in a box. Lived in Bazaar Street. He was a policeman's dog and sometimes sat quietly in a box outside the back door, waiting for the policeman to come home. The policeman never fed him meat, saying it 'made his breath smell'.

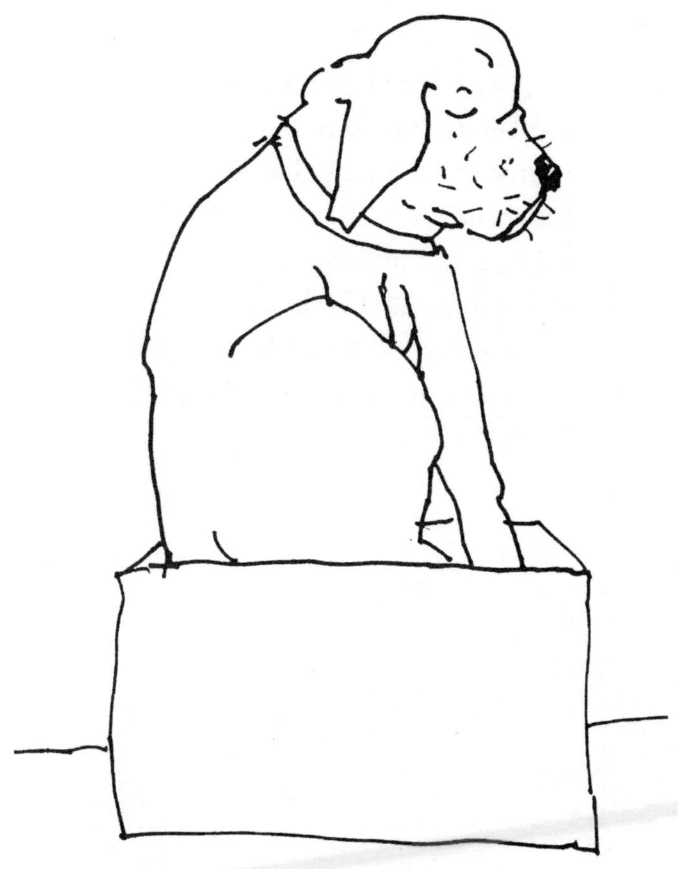

Dog with his Head in a Hole in the Fence. Saw him on the way to my studio every day. Asked his owner why the dog did it. He said he had no idea – he'd been down there and kicked the dog. But the dog persisted for about a year, then never seemed to go back.

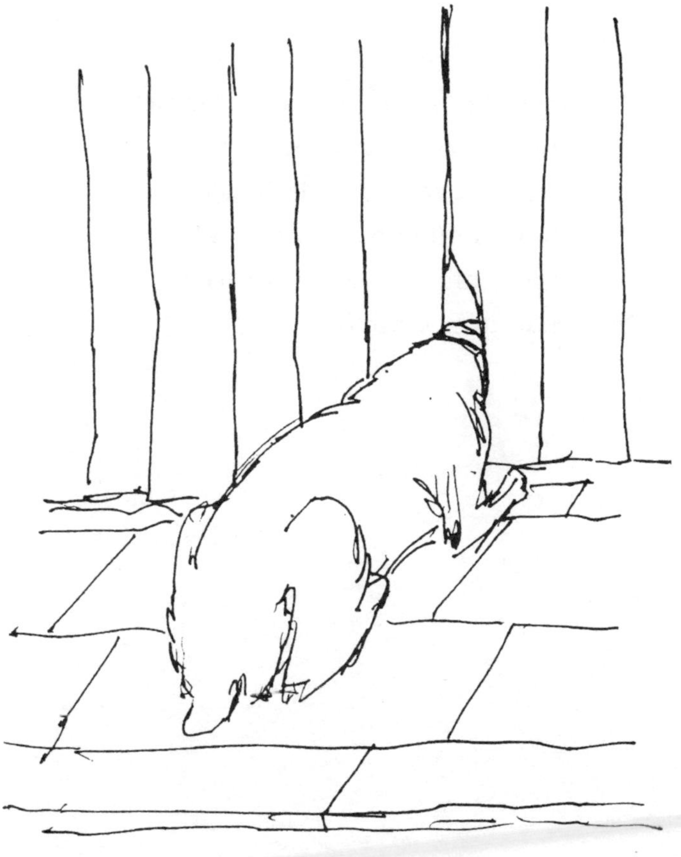

Jago the Sniffer. Lived in the pet shop. Was always shoving his nose between people's legs as they stood at the counter. He didn't mind whether it was a man or a woman.

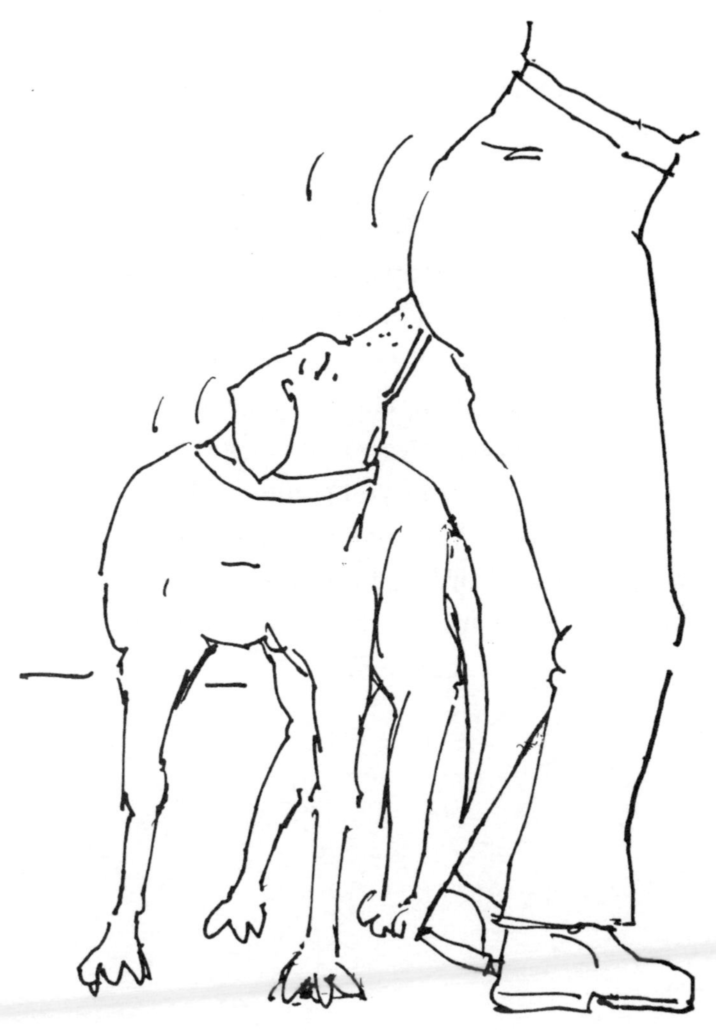

Gilbert, the Newsagent's Dog. Lived in Heap Street. Sat on the shop steps and barked at the customers. Was put down for biting a boy. The newsagent, Mr Shaw, said the boy had tried to kick him and you couldn't blame Gilbert. Was a very affectionate dog according to him – and he missed him so much he never had another dog.

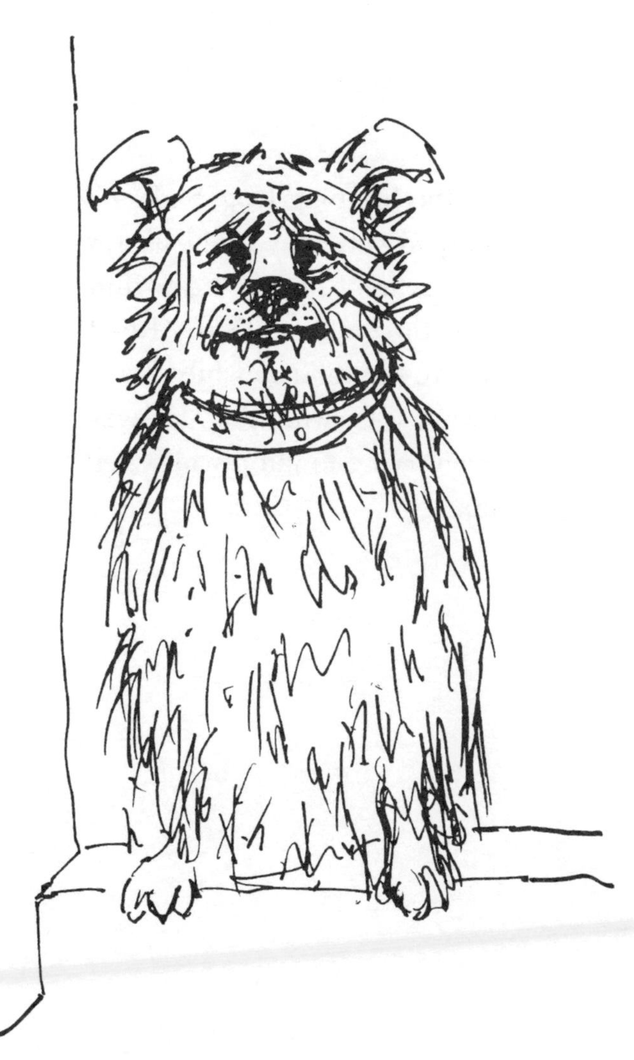

Jip the Jumping Dog. Suddenly jumped vertically in the air for no apparent reason. I saw him near the baths on Derby Road, tied to the railings whilst his owner was swimming. He was even trying to jump whilst tied up.

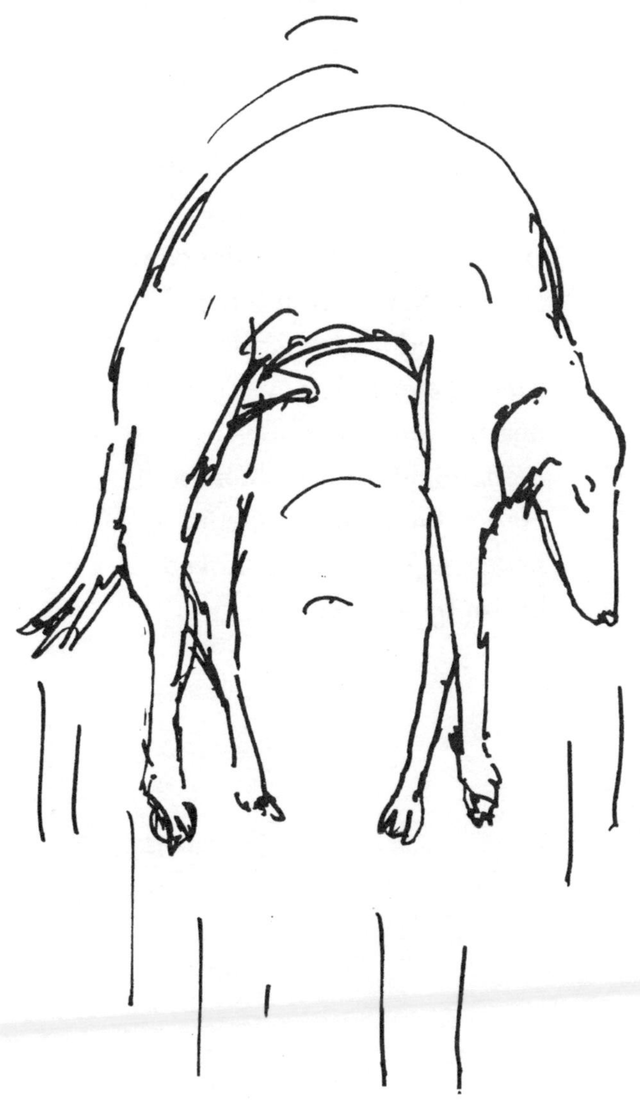

A Thin Dog. Lived in the corner shop in New Barton Street. The owner said it ran very fast. My friend Peter Pilling, who lived nearby, said it had to – because it often had his boot behind it! Had a remarkable appetite – never stopped eating. Loved bacon by all accounts.

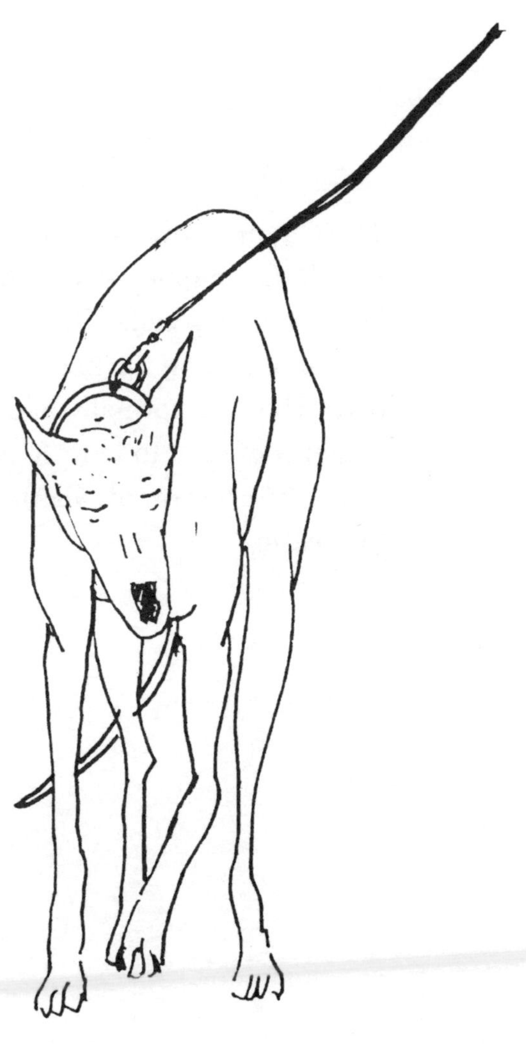

The Chimney Sweep's Dog. Mr Flood, the chimney sweep, had a little white dog called Tom who rode in a box on the back of his bike. The box normally had a bag of soot in it, to fertilise the celery he grew on his allotment in Weaste.

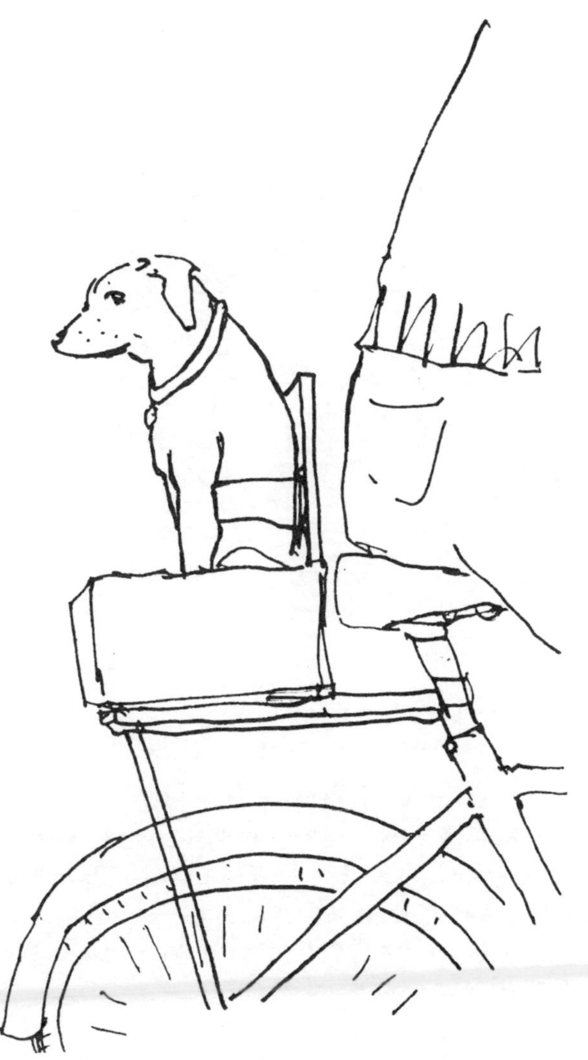

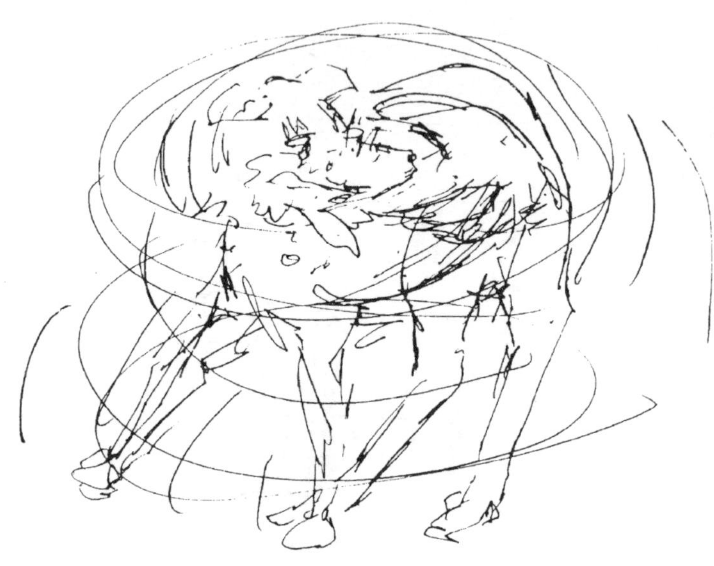

Swinton 1969

'Stick' the thin dog.

was always plagued by flies. Saw him when I was drawing near the Acme mill Swinton. Very thin. The big flies were a pest and he snapped at them - He lived in the House next door to Lowry's old house on Station Road.

About the Artist

Born in Lancashire, where his family has lived for many generations, Harold Riley comes from a long line of artists and musicians who have lived and worked in and around Manchester. He is the third royal portrait painter from the family but has chosen to live all his life where he was born, in the industrial heartland of England.

As a student, he accepted an offer to take part in a scheme to record the city of Salford (a sister city to Manchester) with the artist Laurence Lowry. This record ended at the end of the 20th century and Riley's life's work is being housed in an archive built for it by the city.

Riley is a strong believer in place, believing, as William Wordsworth said, that the child is father of the man. Every aspect of where he lives, the buildings, the people, the sport and the animals, have been his subject all his life.

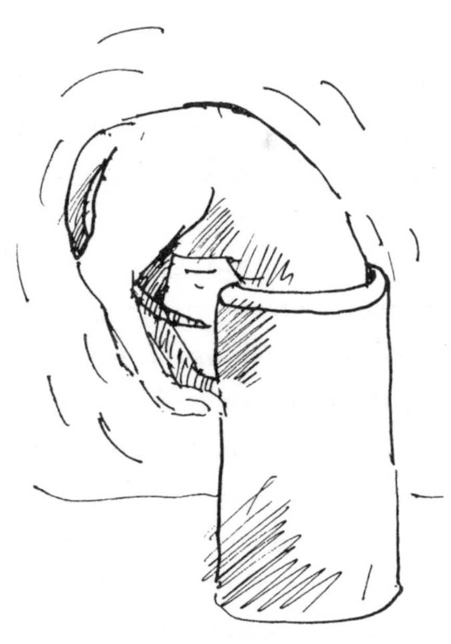

Daft- dog trapped
in grants wood
yard in an
upturned drain.